CW00419153

The Peak District is an upland area at the southern end of the Pennine chain; largely within the borders of Derbyshire, but also crossing into Staffordshire, Cheshire, Greater Manchester and Yorkshire. The greater part of the area is contained within the Peak District National Park (founded 1951). Traditionally, the Peak District is divided into two distinct areas: the northern 'Dark Peak' and the southern 'White Peak'. This book covers the northern area.

The distinction between the two areas is geological. The Dark Peak is based on gritstone and shale, creating a landscape of heather moorland riven by steep-sided valleys. In places, the gritstone breaks through the soil as 'edges': long, low cliffs – such as Stanage Edge *(Walk 19)* and Burbage Rocks *(20)* – much frequented by rock climbers. The population of the area is small; the hills largely empty except for sheep and grouse.

The bulk of the routes described in this guide are in three small areas: the Upper Derwent Valley; the hills around Edale; and the hills and caverns around Castleton.

The Upper Derwent Valley has been dammed to create three large reservoirs – Ladybower, Derwent and Howden – and the lower slopes of the surrounding hills have been planted with conifers. There are short walks through the woodland *(5,8)* and longer walks around the reservoirs *(1,6)* and over the surrounding moors *(2,3,4,7,8,9)*. There are a number of car parks up the length of the valley and a National Park information centre at Fairholmes *(1-5)*.

Edale is a tiny village in the valley of the River Noe. It is famous as the southern end of the Pennine Way, and the southern slopes of the massif of Kinder Scout provide fine hill walking; steep at first, then following level edges marked by dramatic tors *(12,13)*. To the southwest is the long, low ridge of Rushup Edge *(14)*. There is a second information centre at Edale.

Over the ridge to the south is the valley of the River Hope, and the little villages of Hope and Castleton. There is a third information centre at Castleton, which is famous for the ruin of Peveril Castle and the nearby caverns (open to the public) from which the mineral Blue John was extracted *(15)*. To the north of the valley is the ridge which starts with Rushup Edge to the west, then continues along Mam Tor *(16)* – the site of an ancient fort – and on to Lose Hill *(17)*.

The only walks included which are outwith these areas are the climb from Hayfield to Kinder Scout *(10)* – which has possible links with the walks from Edale – and the circuit of little Dale Dike Reservoir, in the low hills above Sheffield *(18)*.

Although there are no large towns in this area, it is dominated by the cities of Sheffield and Manchester which sit to the east and west of the hills. The major line of communication through the area is the A57, which links the two conurbations.

A long, fairly level circuit through mature woodland around two reservoirs, following a quiet public road and clear tracks. Length: **11 miles/18km***; Height Climbed:* **300ft/90m***. Possible links with Walks 3 and 6. Can be cycled.*

O.S. Sheet 110 (OL 1)

To reach the start of this walk, turn off the A57 at the west end of the bridge over Ladybower Reservoir on the road signed for the Derwent Valley. Fairholmes car park is 2¹/₂ miles along the road at the head of the reservoir. There is a National Park information centre in the car park.

Walk back to the roundabout near the entrance to the car park and turn right (ie, heading up the valley). After a short distance, you pass the end of the dramatic Derwent Dam. Follow the quiet public road for a further 4 miles/6.5km beyond this, passing Howden Dam on the way, to reach a turning area for buses (a bus service operates along this stretch on summer weekends) at the end of the road.

Beyond the road end, pass through a gate and continue along a clear track. Follow this for a little under a mile/1.5km, ignoring side paths and following the signs for the cycle route at junctions, to reach the old Derwent packhorse bridge across the river.

Cross the bridge and, on the far side, follow the main track to the left. After a short distance you reach a junction. Double back to the right and follow a clear track all the way back down to Derwent Dam.

A little beyond the dam you join a metalled road. Turn right to return to the start.

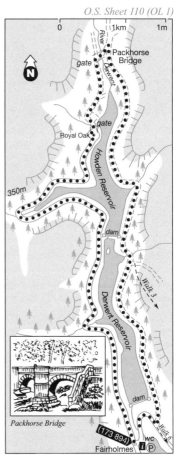

Packhorse Bridge

A steep climb through woodland then an open, ridge-top walk to a dramatic geological feature. The return is along the valleys of the Rivers Alport and Ashop. Length: **8 miles/13km**; *Total Height Climbed:* **870ft/265m**. **NB: take great care with children and animals near cliff edges.**

O.S. Sheet 110 (OL 1)

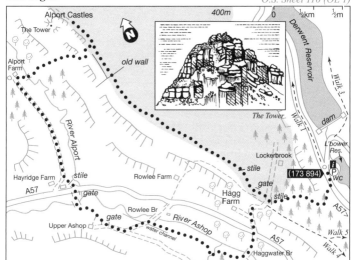

To reach the start of this walk, turn off the A57 at the west end of the bridge over Ladybower Reservoir on the road signed for the Derwent Valley. Fairholmes car park is 2½ miles along the road at the head of the reservoir. There is a National Park information centre in the car park.

Walk a short distance back down the road to a sign pointing right for Hagg Farm. The path climbs through the woods to join a clear track. Turn right. From this point the path is quite clear; contouring then climbing to a stile at the top of the wood.

Once over the stile you are faced by a complex junction of paths and tracks. Go right, on a clear track, but immediately turn left off this, onto a fainter track. This becomes no more than a path as it climbs through grassland to a gate/stile in a wall.

Beyond this, follow a faint path running parallel to the wall to the left. Cross a stile over a fence. Continue straight on beyond for 30m, then edge to the left on a clear path. A wall begins to the left. You start near this but gradually pull away.

The clear path runs to the left of a rounded grassy ridge; eventually becoming flagged, then swinging right and crossing the line of an old wall. Beyond the wall, the path – rougher, but still clear – follows the line of an old wall to the left. By now, the area of landslips called Alport Castles is visible ahead.

You reach the edge of the landslips. After a short distance a clear path doubles back, down to the left. Keep straight on for a short distance, to view The Tower, then double back and take the path downhill.

The next short section is complicated. You join a wall to the right and follow it as it swings right, descending. Then you cross that wall on a stile and continue, with it now to your left. When the wall turns sharp left, you cross a stile and continue, now with a fence to your right. The path gradually pulls away from this fence to join a fence to the left. The path then runs clearly downhill to reach a footbridge over the River Alport.

Turn right on the far side, up the river. After a short distance, a white arrow on a post points up the steep slope to the left to reach a stile over a fence. Cross a field and go through two gates to reach the end of the entrance road to Alport Farm. Turn left and walk down the tarmac road.

Follow this road down the valley for a mile/1.5km until, as it swings right to join the A57, you head off ahead-left to reach a stile, visible below. Follow the path beyond to the road, cross over (carefully), go through a gate and follow a track down to a ford/footbridge.

Beyond the ford, go ahead-left on a clear track. Follow this (ignoring a grass track cutting right to Upper Ashop) to reach a gate/stile in a wall running across the slope. Beyond this you join a metalled road and continue, now with the wall to your left.

At a fork, stay left, on the metalled road (Upper Derwent), and descend to cross a large concrete water channel. Turn right just beyond (Ladybower) to follow a grassy path beside the channel.

When the water disappears into a pipe, continue in the same direction along a flat terrace. When the way becomes blocked, edge to the left, go through a gate and continue.

The path crosses a stream in a tight valley, passing a cylindrical stone building. Shortly beyond, it joins a clear track on the outside of a hairpin bend. Turn left, downhill, to reach a bridge over the River Ashop.

Cross the bridge and follow a clear track up to the A57. Cross over (carefully) and go slightly to the left to reach a sign for a bridleway and the start of a metalled road. Follow this uphill. When it turns left, into Hagg Farm, continue straight on; climbing steeply to return to the complex junction passed before.

Return either by retracing your original route or by following either Walk 4 or Walk 5.

3 Fairholmes & Derwent _____ A

*A circuit which starts by the Derwent Reservoir on a good track, crosses high grazing land on rougher paths, then returns on a quiet public road along Ladybower Reservoir. Length: **6 miles/9.5km**; Height Climbed: **660ft/200m**. Possible links with Walks 1 and 6.*

O.S. Sheet 110 (OL 1)

To reach the start of this walk, turn off the A57 at the west end of the bridge over Ladybower Reservoir on the road signed for the Derwent Valley. Fairholmes car park is 2½ miles along the road at the head of the reservoir. There is a National Park information centre in the car park.

Take the path beyond the information centre and follow it to reach a quiet public road. Turn right along this and cross the river below the massive Derwent Reservoir dam. The dam was completed in 1916, and is best known as the site where 617 Squadron perfected their low-flying techniques for the 'dam busters' raids in 1943. There is a memorial in the dam's west tower.

When the road swings right, away from the dam, two paths cut back to the left. Take the right-hand path (ie, not the one through the gate), which climbs through woodland to join a track near the east tower of the dam. Follow this good track by the side of the reservoir for 1½ miles/2.5km until you reach a sign for a path to Ewden, 'Bradfield & Strines sharp right 40 yards ahead'.

Turn onto the Ewden path. Despite what the sign says, the clearer start to the Bradfield path begins after only 20yds (20m). Turn right here (there is no sign), climbing back and to the right, up and across the wooded slope.

Go through a gate at the top of the wood and continue climbing across an area of moorland, aiming for the left-hand edge of a line of conifers coming up from the wood to the right. At the corner of the wood there is a signpost. Continue in the same direction (Strines), now with an old wall to your right.

As you near a low ruin, below the line of the wall (Bamford House), the path pulls away from the wall.

Follow it to a signposted junction and carry straight on, climbing across the slope to reach a gate/stile at a fence at the highest point of the route.

Looking ahead from the fence you will see a small conifer wood to the left of the line of the path. The path you are on crosses the line of an old wall slightly to the right of that wood, then edges left to follow the line of an old wall to the left.

The path becomes a clear track, edges left when the corner of a wall comes in from the right and descends to a gate/stile in a transverse wall. Beyond this you are in grazing fields. The track passes through one more gate then drops towards the buildings at Lanehead. If you look up to the left at this point you will get a good view of the Salt Cellar – a stone formation on the horizon above Derwent Edge.

At Lanehead you are confronted by three gates. Take the middle gate, which has a yellow arrow on it (the right-hand gate leads into the house and is private). This leads onto a lane, with walls to either side.

There are stiles across this lane, and at one point a path heads off to the left, but there is little doubt about the route: just follow the sunken path straight downhill. At the very bottom it curves to the right to reach a gate/stile leading onto the public road.

Turn right here and follow this quiet public road 1¼ miles/2km back to the start. (NB: A turn to the left at this point links with Walk 6 – an alternative, longer walk back to Fairholmes).

*A steep climb through woods to an open ridge, with a return by Lady-
bower Reservoir. Terrific views. Paths rough and damp in places.
Length: 5¹/₂ miles/9km; Height Climbed: 590ft/180m.*

O.S. Sheet 110 (OL 1)

To reach the start of this walk, turn
off the A57 at the west end of the
bridge over Ladybower Reservoir on
the road signed for the Derwent Valley. This route description starts from
the main car park – Fairholmes – 2¹/₂
miles along the road at the head of the
reservoir. There is a National Park
information centre in the car park.

Look for the sign for the waymarked walks (*see* Walk 5). Follow a
clear path to the road (ignore the steps
to the left) and cross over. On the far
side there is a sign for the waymarked
walks (red, black and green – for the
first part of the walk you will be following the green route).

Go through a gate and climb,
through woodland. You cross a lade

and there is a signposted split. Go
ahead-left (Lockerbrook).

The path climbs to join a forest
track. Turn left along this and follow it round a hairpin bend. Shortly
beyond the bend you turn left, off the
track, and follow a path up to a gate at
the top of the wood.

Beyond the gate, climb through an
open grazing area to reach a T-junc-
tion with a vehicle track. Turn left
along this (green); passing behind the
buildings at Lockerbrook then continuing with a conifer wood to your
left. At the far end of the wood there
is a signposted junction.

Edge to the left, off the track,
and follow a rough path which goes
around the end of the wood (green).

Follow the edge of the trees for ¹/₂ mile/1km to reach a junction. The green walk goes left at this point (a shorter alternative route), but for this walk continue by the wood. The path is now much fainter.

When the trees pull away to the left, keep straight on to reach a gate in a wall, visible ahead. Continue ahead-right from the gate (there is an arrow). When you reach the crown of the field a fine view opens up, and a gate can be seen in a fence ahead.

Beyond the gate, follow a clear path to a gate in the bottom left-hand corner of the field. Here there is a signpost. Go ahead-left (Crookhill Farm). The faint path pulls away from the wall to the right (the route in this section is marked by posts) and eventually drops to join a rough vehicle track with a wall to the left.

As Crookhill Farm appears ahead a sign describes a route bypassing the buildings. A short way before the farm there is a gate to the left and a sign (alternative route). Go through the gate and head diagonally across the field to reach a gate onto a lane.

Turn left down the lane to reach the public road, then turn left, passing a bus turning area. A short distance beyond, a path cuts back and to the right, dropping through the trees to join the path by the reservoir. Turn left along this to return to Fairholmes.

5 Fairholmes Short Walks _____ B/C

Three waymarked walks starting from the information centre and car park, leading through woods and to the dramatic Derwent Dam.

These routes are well marked and easy to follow, but that does not mean they are easy. All three begin up a steep slope, and if you are not fit you should try the shortest – red – route first, just to get a feel for the gradient.

The first part of the walks is described in Walk 4.

Red: A short climb, then across the slope to Derwent Dam.
Length: **1 mile/1.5km**; *Climb:* **100ft/30m.**

Black: A longer climb through trees, then zig-zag back down a forest track to return *via* Derwent Dam.
Length: **2 miles/3km**; *Climb:* **525ft/160m.**

Green: A longer climb through trees, then along a rough path on an open ridge for a short distance before dropping back down through the

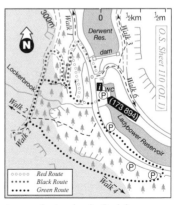

trees and returning by Ladybower Reservoir.
Length: **3 miles/4.5km**; *Climb:* **525ft/160m.**

A walk around the upper part of Ladybower Reservoir, following quiet public roads and good paths. Length: **6 miles/9.5km**; *Height Climbed:* negligible. *Possible links with Walks 1, 3 & 7.*

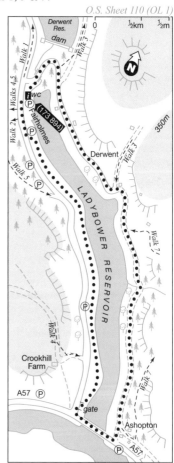

O.S. Sheet 110 (OL 1)

This route takes the walker around the northern arm of Ladybower Reservoir – the section to the north of the bridge carrying the A57. The route can be joined at a number of points, and there are numerous possible parking places (*see* map). In the following description, it is assumed that you have started from the pay car park at Fairholmes – at the north end of the reservoir and reached by the public road which runs up the western side.

From beyond the information centre in the car park, follow the clear path which leads to a quiet public road. Turn right along this, crossing the River Derwent below the dramatic Derwent Dam then swinging right to run down the far side of Ladybower Reservoir.

When the road ends, continue on a clear track which follows the shore of the reservoir down to Ashopton, at the east end of the bridge carrying the A57.

Turn right, across the bridge (there is a pavement). At the end of the bridge, swing right. After a short distance you reach a gate and a sign for the concession footpath to Fairholmes. The path starts through an open field then enters the trees above the reservoir. After 2 miles/3km the path joins the road. Turn right to return to the car park.

A climb through woodland and moorland, returning by the side of a reservoir. Length: 4¹/₂ miles/7km; Height Climbed: 525ft/160m. Rough paths; fine views.

O.S. Sheet 110 (OL 1)

Park by the road at Ashopton – at the east end of the bridge where the A57 crosses Ladybower Reservoir.

Walk towards the bridge but turn right onto a metalled road shortly before it. At a junction, double back to the right and continue along this road/track, ignoring entrances to either side, until you approach a transverse wall with a gate in it.

Just before this gate there is another gate, to the left, and a sign for Whinstone Lee Tor. Go through this. A clear path beyond quickly joins a wall to the left and runs through the trees, then on, following the wall, over open ground, before turning right and climbing to a complex junction of paths on a low col.

Turn left here, onto the ridge, and follow a clear path, passing rocky outcrops, for half a mile/1km to reach a signposted junction by a line of grouse butts. Go left (Derwent).

The path descends to a wall running across the slope. Turn right along this for 70m, then turn left through a gate (Derwent).

A clear path runs diagonally across the field, aiming for the right-hand edge of a conifer wood. Pass through a gate in a wall on the edge of the wood and continue with trees to your left and a wall to your right.

Go through a gate at the end of the trees and follow a clear path through fields; dropping to cross Grindle Clough and then climbing to a group of old stone farm buildings. Go through the gate which allows you to pass between them (the first building on the right is now a shelter), turning left after the first building to reach a gate.

Beyond the gate a clear path runs down a field to join a track above the reservoir. Turn left along this (*see Walk 6*) to return to the start.

Three waymarked walks through the woods above Ladybower Reservoir. Possible extension from the longest route to a fine viewpoint. Length: 1-3¾ miles/1.5-6km (add ¾ mile/1km to longest route for climb to Win Hill); Height Climbed: 70-820ft/20-250m.

O.S. Sheet 110 (OL 1)

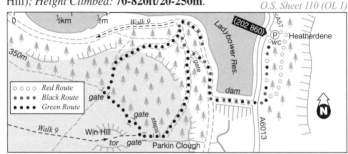

Heatherdene car park is to the east of Ladybower Reservoir, just south of the A57/A6013 junction. The waymarked walks run south from the car park (ie, through the disabled section), following the path for Ladybower Dam. The routes are well marked by red, black and green arrows.

When the path is almost level with the dam it splits. **For the shortest route (red)** go left and double back to the car park through pleasant mature woodland. **For the longer routes,** cross the A6013 and continue across the dam. At the far end turn right on a clear track by the reservoir.

After a short distance, go left on a clear path (green/black). The path climbs through trees then runs level to reach a pedestrian gate. Immediately beyond this there is a junction.

For the shorter route (black) turn right; descending to the shore track and turning right to return to the start.

For the longer walk (green), go left. The clear path runs across the slope to reach the steep, narrow valley of Parkin Clough. Turn right, climbing steps at first. The path climbs to a fence with a gate in it. Just beyond there is a signposted junction.

To reach Win Hill, go straight uphill from the signpost; climbing out of the trees then over moorland to reach the dramatic tor with its splendid views.

To continue with the green route, turn right (Ladybower), with a wall to your left. Go through a gate at the end of the trees, and continue with trees to your right and moorland to your left (Ladybower).

At a signposted four-way junction, go right (Ladybower), through a gate and into the trees. Follow the green arrows at three junctions to reach the track by the reservoir. Turn right to return to the start.

A clear track along the shore of Ladybower Reservoir, with a return along a Roman road along an open ridge. Terrific views. Length: **9 miles/14.5km**; *Height Climbed:* **820ft/250m.**

O.S. Sheet 110 (OL 1)

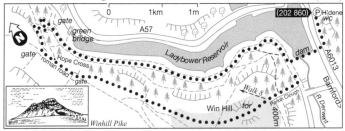

Start this walk from the Heatherdene car park, on the east side of Ladybower Reservoir just south of the A57/A6013 junction.

At the south end of the coach parking area there is a sign for Ladybower dam. Follow the path (Win Hill is visible to your right) to a road crossing point, level with the dam.

Cross the dam. At the far end, turn right (concession bridleway) on a clear track through the woodland by the reservoir. Follow this clear, pleasant track, ignoring all paths leading off to the left, for 3½ miles/5.5km.

You pass the head of the reservoir. Shortly beyond, a green metal bridge becomes visible, crossing the river to your right. At the signposted junction here, keep left, up the slope (ie, don't cross the bridge).

After a short distance a signposted path cuts off to the left. Stay on the clearer, right-hand path and follow it to a gate leading to a junction with a rough track.

Turn left, up the track. Beyond a gate, the trees end to the right; after another they end to the left, and the track climbs through grassland to a junction on the ridge ahead. Turn left, through a gate. You are now on the line of the Roman road.

Follow the path through two gates. Beyond the second there is a split. Go ahead-left here; climbing to rejoin the edge of the trees on the top of the ridge. Stick to the ridge now, ignoring paths to right and left, to reach the rocky tor of Winhill Pike at the top of Win Hill.

Walk along the summit ridge (the views are superb) and follow the well-maintained path straight on down the other side; passing through a wall, entering the woodland, and following a steep path – with steps in places – down Parkin Clough.

Go straight on at all junctions until you reach the clear track a short way above the River Derwent. Turn left here to return to the dam.

*A classic hill route: through a wooded valley, past a reservoir, then onto
the western edge of Kinder Scout. Paths rough and steep in places;
views terrific. Length:* **9 miles/14.5km**; *Height Climbed:* **1,380ft/420m.**

O.S. Sheet 110 (OL 1)

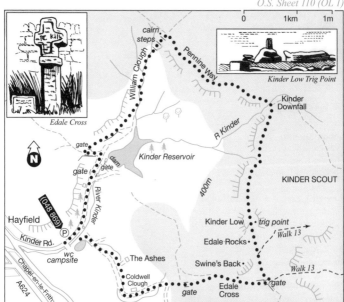

Edale Cross

Kinder Low Trig Point

This walk starts from the picturesque
little village of Hayfield, midway
between Glossop and Chapel-en-le-
Frith on the A624. From the centre
of the village, look for the sign for
the campsite. This leads onto Kinder
Road. Drive (or walk) a little under
a mile/1.5km up this road, up the
valley of the River Kinder, to reach
Bowden Bridge car park (to the left of
the road).

Start walking up the road beyond

the car park (ie, don't cross the bridge
opposite the car park entrance; that
is your return route). Ignoring house
entrances to the right of the road, continue up the pleasant wooded valley
until you reach the entrance gate for
Kinder Reservoir. A footpath crosses
a bridge to the right at this point, but
for this route keep straight on, following the entrance road to the left of the
river (concession bridleway).

You reach a second gate (no public

access). Immediately to the left of the gate is the start of a cobbled track (bridleway). Follow this track, uphill at first, until you are almost level with the end of the dam to your right. Two walls come in from the left at this point, the first at an acute angle. Turn back-left here, following the clear path by the first wall.

The path climbs to a gate in a wall running across the slope. Go through this and turn right (signed for Snake Inn and Edale on the post just beyond), with the wall to your right.

Near the head of the reservoir, the wall turns downhill to the right and there is a split in the path. Keep straight on, contouring at first then descending to join the stream in William Clough. The path follows the stream up the little valley, crossing and re-crossing several times. Near the top, the valley splits. Keep right. Shortly beyond, the path becomes a flight of stone steps and climbs to a junction by a loose cairn, just short of the watershed.

Turn right here, following a paved path over a damp area then climbing a steep slope. You are now on the Pennine Way, and a clear path runs along the edge for $1^1/2$ miles/2.5km to the rocky gully of Kinder Downfall, where the River Kinder drops over the edge of the boggy plateau of Kinder Scout. Cross the river. A path heads off to the left at this point (for Edale), but for this route continue along the edge.

Stick to the main path and, after a little over a mile/1.5km, you reach the trig point at Kinder Low. Navigation can be a little tricky at this point (the soil erosion is very bad just here: please stick to paths to avoid making it worse), with a number of possible paths. Continue in the direction you were going before and, just beyond the top, the rocky outcrop of Edale Rocks will become visible ahead, with the clear path passing to the left.

The path continues to descend, passing the end of the grassy Swine's Back then dropping to a four-way junction by the corner of a wall.

Turn right here, passing through a gate in one wall and continuing with the other to your right. After a short distance you pass through a gap in another wall. Immediately beyond you will see the medieval Edale Cross to your right.

Continue on the clear track with the wall to your right, ignoring a path cutting off to the right, to reach a metal gate at the top of a lane between fences. Continue down this (ignoring a second path off to the right) to reach the end of the metalled road.

There is a split immediately. Keep right, crossing a stream. The road passes the old farm buildings at Coldwell Clough, swings to the right and splits again. Keep right (walkers only).

You join the access road to The Ashes farm. Keep straight on here and continue to a bridge over the River Sett. On the far side there is a junction: go left and follow the road by the river back down to the junction by the car park.

Walks North Peak District

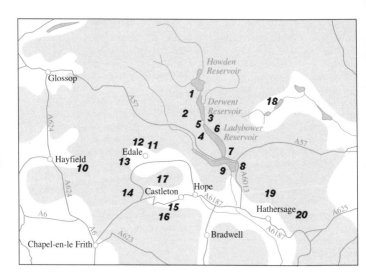

Grades

A ...... Full walking equipment required

B ...... Strong walking footwear and waterproof clothing required

C ...... Comfortable walking footwear recommended

[B/C, etc ...... Split grades refer to multiple route titles]

—— www.pocketwalks.com ——

Published by: Hallewell Publications, The Milton,
Foss, Pitlochry, Perthshire PH16 5NQ
Printed by: J. Thomson Printers, Glasgow

Walks North Peak District

While every care has been taken in the preparation of this guide, the publishers cannot accept responsibility for any loss, damage or injury resulting from its use.

Two circuits leading to the hills behind Edale. **11)** *A short climb to a viewpoint a little above the farmland. Length:* **3 miles/5km;** *Height Climbed:* **625ft/190m.** **12)** *A steep climb leading to a moorland walk along a rocky edge. Length:* **7 miles/11km;** *Height Climbed:* **1,200ft/ 360m.**

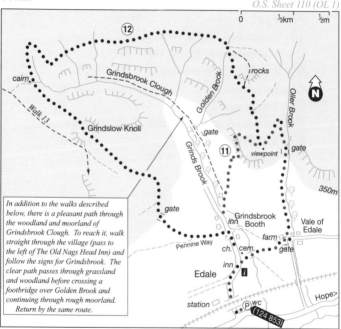

O.S. Sheet 110 (OL 1)

In addition to the walks described below, there is a pleasant path through the woodland and moorland of Grindsbrook Clough. To reach it, walk straight through the village (pass to the left of The Old Nags Head Inn) and follow the signs for Grindsbrook. The clear path passes through grassland and woodland before crossing a footbridge over Golden Brook and continuing through rough moorland. Return by the same route.

Walks 11 & 12) Start from the large car park by the road junction just south of Edale Station. From the car park, follow the signs for the footpath to Edale. This leads onto the minor road. Turn right along this, passing the station and the Moorland Centre (information) before turning right at a sign for a footpath just before the cemetery.

Cross a bridge over a stream. Just beyond there is a gate, with a signposted junction immediately beyond. Go straight on here, walking along the edge of a field with a fence to your left.

Beyond the end of the field you continue in the same direction, now with a wall to your right. This leads to a farm. Keep right at the junction amongst the farm buildings; passing through a gate to reach a junction with the public road.

Look for a sign for a footpath to open country to the left. This is an access route, marked by white arrows. You enter a field and edge over to the right-hand side, then climb through three fields, with the trees around Oller Brook to your right, to reach a gate at the edge of the access land.

Immediately beyond the gate the track splits. Keep to the left; following the stream for a short distance and then doubling back to the left, climbing up and across the slope.

The path passes a fine viewpoint just before reaching a junction with a clearer path.

Walk 11) For the shorter route, turn left here. The path zig-zags down the slope to reach a gate in a wall at the bottom of a stand of trees. Go through the gate and follow the path down to a junction with the path up Grindsbrook Clough (*see* map for description of this path). For this route, turn left. The path swings right and drops to cross Grinds Brook. Climb the slope on the far side and turn left at the junction with a track to return to the start.

Walk 12) For the longer route, turn right. The path now climbs steeply, with a fine view of Grinds-brook Clough to the left and a rocky outcrop directly ahead. The path splits twice: keep left both times (if you keep right at the second split it will lead you over the rocky outcrop and back to the main path – *see* map).

Beyond the outcrop the path continues climbing until it reaches the ridge. Turn left along a clear, slab path along the ridge, with heather moorland scattered with tors to your right and a fine view to the south.

After 1½ miles/2.5km the path reaches a deep valley rising from the head of Grindsbrook Clough. It heads sharply right, to go round the head of the valley, then doubles back down the other side. Shortly beyond a loose cairn there is a split in the path, with a well-maintained path heading off to the right and a rougher path going left, aiming for the peak of Grindslow Knoll at the end of a ridge. Go left.

From the top of Grindslow Knoll, go left on a rough path which heads roughly for the steeple of the church in Edale (Grindsbrook Booth). The path winds downhill – there is no doubt about the route – until it reaches a gate/stile in a wall.

Cross the stile and you are in a field. A faint path leads down to the bottom right-hand corner of the field (you are heading roughly towards some large sheds), where you go through a gap in a wall, with a small stream to your right.

Continue by the stream and you reach a signposted junction with the Pennine Way. Keep straight on here to follow a lane down into the village.

You join the street opposite the Old Nags Head inn – the southern end of the Pennine Way. To return to the start of this walk, turn right.

A steep climb onto the moors via a flight of steps (Jacob's Ladder), a rough path through the extraordinary tors on the south edge of Kinder Scout, and a return through moorland and farmland. Paths rough and wet in places and some navigation may be required – particularly if it is misty. Length: **6½ miles/10.5km**; Height Climbed: **1,200ft/370m**.

O.S. Sheet 110 (OL 1)

Footbridge below Jacob's Ladder

KINDER SCOUT

Pennine Way
Walk 10
Pym Chair
Wool Packs
Noe Stool
cairn
Swine's Back
wall
gate
Walk 10
Jacob's Ladder
Crowden Clough
Crowden Brook
small tor
Walk 12
Grindslow Knoll
pools
Wool Packs
Pennine Way
Lee Farm
stile
Edale
Pennine Way
River Noe
Upper Booth
500m
N
(108 847)
Walk 14
P
Hope
Barber Booth

To reach the start of this walk, follow the road up Edale (its eastern end is in the village of Hope). At the west end of the valley is the little village of Barber Booth. Here, turn on to the minor road to Upper Booth. Follow the road under the railway line and

park in the car park just beyond.

Walk on up the public road, which ends at the hamlet of Upper Booth. Here, there is a signposted junction of paths. Go straight on (Jacob's Ladder) – you are now on the Pennine Way. Immediately, you cross a bridge over Crowden Brook. Just beyond, a path heads off to the right. Ignore this and stick to the main track.

Follow the track straight through the buildings at Lee Farm and continue. After a further half a mile/1km, the track swings right to reach a stone bridge over a little river. The stone steps of Jacob's Ladder are visible beyond (as is the line of a track, heading off to the left, which makes a gentler ascent of the same slope).

Climb the steps (or the track). A more level path continues beyond – initially with a broken-down wall to the right and the river in the valley beyond. This eventually reaches the corner of a wall, coming in from the left, with a gate in it. Here, there is a signposted junction.

Go right here (Pennine Way), climbing gently to the line of an old wall along the foot of a rocky hill (Swine's Back).

Descend by the wall to reach a junction by a large, loose cairn. A sign indicates that the Pennine Way heads off to the left, but for this walk keep straight on. The path is clear but there is no sign.

The next section of the path – which is fragmented and very boggy and wet in places – is notable for some spectacular rock formations. The path starts by heading northeast by the old wall. After passing the Noe Stool, the wall drops away to the right and the path heads east, passing Pym Chair and then running through the bizarre tors known as the Wool Packs. Beyond these it edges

to the left to round the narrow head of Crowden Clough. Beyond this the path, along the top of the slope, becomes much easier to follow.

Half a mile/1km beyond Crowden Clough, the path reaches a small tor with distinctive twin tops. At this point there is a split. The main path – slabbed and very clear – heads off ahead-left. For this route, however, go right on a clear, rough path.

The path, along the flat top of a ridge, is very wet in places and can become indistinct. If in doubt, aim to the right of the mound (Grindslow Knoll) at the end of the ridge.

Once level with the mound, the path swings to the right (almost due south) and begins to descend through grassland. Just beyond the Knoll there is a split. Keep right here (ie, straight on).

The path passes to the left of a small pool, then two larger ones become visible to the left. Keep straight on, and in a short distance you will reach a broken-down wall running across the slope. The path passes through the wall slightly to the right of a second wall, which runs on straight ahead. Follow this second wall down a very steep slope.

As you descend, you will notice the route of the Pennine Way ahead: a clear footpath crossing the fields below. The path you are on comes down to a stile over a fence. Cross this and join the Pennine Way path, just beyond. Turn right to return to Upper Booth, then retrace your steps to the car park.

This walk starts through farmland before climbing steeply onto an open ridge, then returning through farmland. Terrific views. Length: **5 miles/8km**; *Height Climbed:* **950ft/290m**. *It is possible to extend the walk along the ridge to Lose Hill (see Walks 16 & 17).*

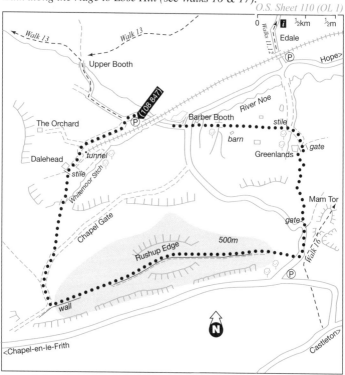

To reach the start of this walk, follow the instructions given for Walk 13.

From the car park, walk a short way along the road in the direction of Upper Booth then turn left at the sign for Dalehead. Follow the clear access road, which swings to the right then runs straight for a while before splitting.

Keep left at the split and follow the track to Dalehead Farm, where there is an information shelter. At the far end of the buildings there is a stile leading into a field and a signpost.

Go ahead-left (Chapel Gate). Cross the field to reach a gate (it is a little marshy under foot at first), then continue in the same direction to reach a wall with a stile over it. A yellow arrow points half-right. This leads to the far corner of the field, where there is a stone stile leading into the trees around Whitemoor Sitch.

The path leads a short distance upstream to reach a plank bridge. Cross this and climb the grassy slope ahead. The path can be faint but there is no doubt about the route: straight uphill to join the Chapel Gate track.

Turn right (Chapel-en-le-Frith), following the track up and across the slope. When you get to the highest point of the ridge, a path cuts back and to the right. Ignore this and continue on the main track to join a clear track running beside a well-maintained stone wall. Turn left (Castleton).

After a short distance there is a gate in the wall to the right. The bridleway goes through the gate and continues to the right of the wall. This is the route taken by cyclists; if you are walking, keep to the left.

Follow the ridge for 1$^1/_2$ miles/ 2.5km – the views are splendid on this stretch – to reach a road crossing a dip in the ridge. If you wish to make a diversion at this point, Mam Tor is directly ahead, with the ridge extending beyond (see Walks 16 & 17). For this route, however, cross

the road and turn left for a short distance to reach a gate to your right. There are signs for two bridleways here: take the left-hand one, starting parallel to the road.

The clear path runs down the hill to reach the buildings at Greenlands. Swing to the right here. Just beyond the buildings, go left, through a gate, to join the access road to the house. Turn right along this.

The metalled road crosses a stream. Just beyond this you turn left, off the road; climbing a set of stone steps to reach a stile. Walk straight across a field to reach a gate on the far side. You are now in a sequence of grazing fields. Walk straight across four of them.

At the end of the fourth field you go down some stone steps to cross a stream then climb more steps on the far side to enter a field with a barn in it. A yellow arrow points straight ahead. Aim to join a broken-down wall with trees along it which comes up from the right.

The route now passes through the line of the wall and continues (the way is marked by posts here, so it is quite easy to follow); descending to a plank bridge over a stream. Climb up the other side. The path now runs between a hedge/fence to the left and a single-strand wire fence to the right.

Cross another stile and a stream then continue straight ahead to join the public road at Barber Booth. You join the road at a junction. Walk up the road opposite to return to the start of the walk.

A walk leading past the entrances to the four show caves around Castleton (there is a fee for entry to each of them) and the dramatic landslip below Mam Tor, and returning through farmland. Length: **4 miles/6.5km**; *Height Climbed:* **490ft/150m**.

O.S. Sheet 110 (OL 1)

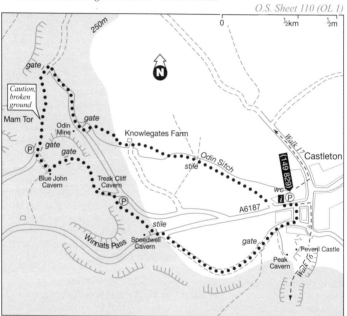

Park in the car park in the centre of Castleton. Walk out of the entrance and turn left, along Cross St, then right (up Castle St) at the sign for Peveril Castle.

At the top of Castle St there is a junction. If you go half-right at this point you will reach the entrance to Peveril Castle. To continue with this walk, however, turn right.

Where the road crosses the Peakshole Water a path leads to the left up to the first of the caverns: Peak Cavern. Make a diversion if you wish to visit the cave, but otherwise keep straight on along a street called Goosehill.

Continue straight along the road (ignoring a footpath signed to the left); out of the houses and on to a gate in a wall. Go through the gate and continue, with a wall to the right and the open fell up to your left, until you join the public road near the entrance to the dramatic Winnats Pass.

Cross the road (carefully) and turn left for a short distance to reach a gate/stile to the right. At this point, the entrance to Speedwell Cavern – the second cave – is visible just ahead. To continue with the walk, however, go right, over the stile.

Follow a rough path through grassland to a gate/stile. Beyond this the path continues across the slope, initially with a wall to the right, until it joins a concrete track climbing up from a car park by the road below. Turn left up this, climbing towards the entrance to the third cavern: Treak Cliff Cavern.

Walk up the left-hand side of the buildings – past the entrance to the shop, tea room, etc – then climb above them. A sign (footpath) points right and you walk along behind the buildings then continue on a rough path up and across the grassy slope.

Climb up to the corner of the field, with gates ahead and to the right. Go straight on and follow a clear path to the entrance to the last of the caves: Blue John Cavern (this is named after the mineral called Blue John: a blue and yellow fluorspar found only in this area in Britain).

Follow the cavern's tarmac driveway up to the public road and turn right. There is room for parking and then a gate, marking the end of the road. Continue beyond this, on what

was a road until it had to be closed in 1979 following a number of landslides. It is still walkable, but care must be taken at this stage. The evidence of the landslides – the scarred face of Mam Tor and the broken ground beneath – is very dramatic.

Beyond the broken area, go through a gate and double back to the right. Follow the tarmac road past the interpretation board about the landslides and the entrance to the old Odin lead mine. Just beyond this there is a gate to the left.

Go through the gate and you are in a slightly confusing area amongst the old lead workings. Cross a small stream and follow the clear path beyond, with the stream on your right. This leads you down to a stile above Knowlegates Farm.

Cross the stile and follow the path round to the front of the farm, where there is a signposted junction. Go straight on (Castleton), passing through a pedestrian gate and continuing with a small stream to your right. Beyond the next gate, continue directly across a field.

At the far side of the field cross a stile over a wall, then cross the corner of a field to a further stile, by a gate. Cross a small concrete bridge immediately beyond and continue, now with a fence to your left.

Go straight across a tarmac road at the end of the field, cross a stile and continue, with a fence to your left and the stream beyond that. From this point, the path into Castleton is straightforward.

A circuit which starts up a narrow, rocky dale, then continues through farmland to reach a summit ringed by the remains of an ancient fort.
Length: **5¹/2 miles/9km**; *Height Climbed:* **1,100ft/330m**. *Possible links with walks 14 and 17.*

O.S. Sheet 110 (OL 1)

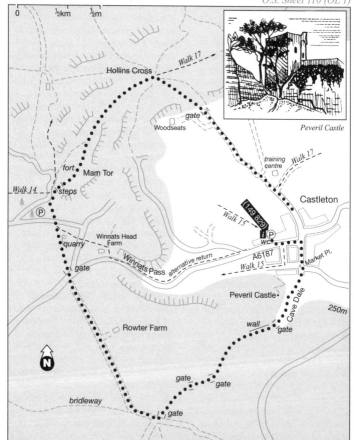

Peveril Castle

Park in the car park in the centre of the village of Castleton. Walk out of the entrance to the car park and turn left along Cross Street. When the street turns hard to the left you go right (sign for Cave Dale) and follow the street to the triangular open area at Market Place.

Take the left-hand road out of Market Place. After a short distance, turn right at the sign for Cave Dale; starting between houses then continuing on a rough, rocky path up the narrow, grassy dale. There are a number of caves in the dale, and good views of the dramatic ruin of Peveril Castle (access to the castle is from the village) at the top of the slope to your right.

At the top of the dale a wall with a gate in it crosses the way. Go through the gate and continue with a wall to your right. Follow the path by the wall (ignoring smaller paths cutting off) for a little over half a mile/1km to reach a transverse wall with a gate in it. Go through this and follow a clear path across a field to reach a second gate. Just beyond this a post points half-left and a grassy path leads to a gate in the top right-hand corner of a large field.

The gate leads onto a track between walls. Turn right along this, passing through a gate. A short distance beyond the gate there is a split, with a bridleway carrying straight on and the main track going right. Go right here and follow the clear track down to the public road.

Cross the road (take care). There is a gate directly opposite: ignore this and look for one just to the right, with a sign for a footpath at it. Go through this gate and follow a clear path past an old quarry and up to the road. (Shortly before you reach the road a path heads off to the right. This is the start of a possible short cut back to Castleton: joining the public road by Winnats Head Farm and then following a path by the road through Winnats Pass and back to the start – *see* map.)

Cross the road (carefully), aiming slightly to the left, to reach another gate. Follow a clear path up the slope beyond to join a road as it approaches a gap in a ridge. Just before joining the road you bear right onto the stone steps leading up the slope of Mam Tor.

Pass through the earth walls of the old fort (associated with the Celtic peoples who lived here some 3,000 years ago) and climb to the summit, then continue along the ridge until you reach the junction by the little monument at Hollins Cross, at the lowest point of the ridge.

If you wish to link this walk with Walk 17 then continue along the ridge. **If you wish to complete this circuit**, go half ahead-right at the junction: descending across the slope on a good, clear path to reach a gate/stile at the top of a lane.

Go through a further gate/stile at the foot of the lane, then continue straight ahead, down the quiet public road through farmland, to return to Castleton.

17 **Hollins Cross, Back Tor & Lose Hill** _____ **B**

A circuit, on rough paths and quiet public roads, climbing to a ridge.
Splendid views. Length: **4¹/₂ miles/7km**; *Height Climbed:* **950ft/290m**.
Possible link with Walk 16.

O.S. Sheet 110 (OL 1)

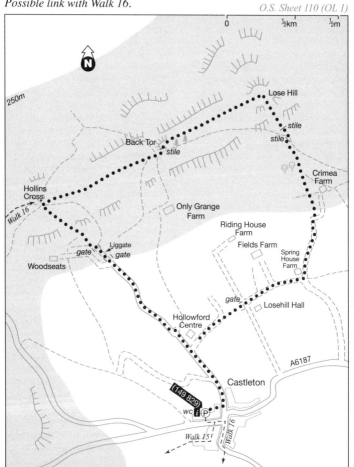

Park in the car park in the centre of the little village of Castleton. At the back, right-hand corner of the car park a track begins. Follow this to a junction with a street and turn left (sign for Edale).

Follow the street out of the village. At a fork there is a sign to the right for the Hollowford Centre. This is the return route, but for now keep left. A short distance beyond, a track cuts off to the right (footpath). Ignore this and stick to the main, metalled road.

As you approach the foot of the hills there is a further junction. Keep straight on here (Hollins Cross) to reach a gate/stile. Beyond this, a narrow lane (Liggate) leads between fields to a further gate/stiles and a signposted junction. Go left (foot-path). The path is rough at first, up and across the slope, but becomes a slab path with steps as it approaches the top of the ridge.

There is a complex junction of paths on the ridge (and a possible link with walk 16). For this route turn right, following a clear, rough path along the top of the ridge. After half a mile/1km you reach the low point before the rocky outcrop of Back Tor. Cross a stile to the left and follow the rough path to the top of the Tor (be careful near the edge) then on along the ridge. Continue for a further half mile/1km to reach the top of Lose Hill, at the end of the ridge.

Swing right from the top, follow-ing a well-made path down to a stile over a fence. Beyond this there is a junction. Go right, crossing a stile over a fence and continuing with the fence to your left. Just beyond a line of trees to the right, as you approach a farm, there is a junction.

Go right here (Castleton) and follow a grassy path down to a small gate at the right-hand end of a stone wall. Go through the gate and continue down the right-hand side of the field below. Keep straight on at the signposted junction half-way down the field. Beyond the gate/stile at the foot of the field you join a track where it makes a right-angled bend. Go straight on along this track.

Follow the track down to Spring House Farm. The track passes to the left of the main house and then reaches a junction. Go right here (Castleton).

After a short way you reach a junction of tracks. Ignore the track heading right, to a farm, and continue on the other track, heading for the buildings at Losehill Hall. Just beyond the Hall the track swings hard left. At this point there is a gate to the right – the entrance to Riding House Farm – with a smaller, pedestrian, gate just to the left of it marked by a sign for a footpath. Go through the pedestrian gate and walk on with a wall to your right.

Pass through another gate, and over some stepping stones immedi-ately beyond. A faint path crosses the field beyond to reach a gate leading onto a track. Turn left along this to reach the Hollowford Centre and then the junction with the original road.

Turn left to return to the start.

A walk through the woodland around a small reservoir. Paths rough and damp in places. Length: **3¹/₂ miles/5.5km**; *Height Climbed: up to* **295ft/90m**.

O.S. Sheet 110 (OL 1)

Dale Dike is one of the reservoirs in the hills to the north-west of Sheffield. To reach it, turn north off the A57 about 2 miles east of Ladybower Reservoir (Strines Moor) and follow the minor roads. There are three possible parking places (*see* map). The route is described from the small parking area above Strines Reservoir, ³/₄ mile north of Strines Inn.

Walk down the vehicle track which starts by the parking area, with a wood to your left. The track leads down to the house at Brogging, at the end of the dam for Strines Reservoir.

Turn right just beyond Brogging and follow a path which descends, with the grass wall of the dam up to your right, to enter an area of woodland.

Continue through the trees to reach two footbridges over a bend in a river. Cross both and follow the clear path beyond, down the side of the reservoir to the dam at the far end.

Go round the end of the wall which has run along the dam and continue on a clear track for a short distance to reach a junction with another track. Turn right here (a turn to the left leads to the Dale Dike car park).

You descend to a footbridge below a concrete weir. Cross that and climb some stone steps. These lead you to a path which runs past the end of the dam and on along the side of the reservoir.

After a short way you reach a signposted junction. Go straight on (Yorkshire Water Permissive Footpath – the path to the left leads to the Blindside Lane car park). The path becomes rougher and damper, but there is no doubt about the route back to the head of the reservoir.

A walk above and below the crags of the most famous of the Peak District 'Edges'. Rough paths through open country. Fine views. Length: **5 miles/8km**; *Height Climbed:* **490ft/150m**. *No dogs.*

O.S. Sheet 110 (OL 1)

The dramatic crags of Stanage Edge – a favourite haunt of rock climbers – can be accessed from a number of points. To reach the car park for this walk, turn onto School Lane from the centre of the village of Hathersage. After 1¹/₂ miles, turn left onto a minor road. After ¹/₂ mile turn right at a junction on the edge of a wood. The car park (fee) is a short way along this road on the right-hand side.

A path starts from the back of the car park. Follow this across an area of open ground and into a wood. At the top of the wood (fine view of the crags from here) there are two paths. Go straight on (bridleway) along the clearer path; passing the right-hand end of a wall then clambering through the crags to join a path along the top.

The crags stretch in either direction, and it is possible to make a detour to the right from here. For this route, however, go left. After a short distance, the main path (Long Causeway) edges down and across the slope. Turn onto a smaller path here to continue along the top.

Follow the path past a trig point, round the bend at Crow Chin and on to the tiny, disued quarry at Stanage End. Turn left on a track through some old walls, then left again on a faint path back along the foot of the crags – by this point very low.

After 1¹/₂ miles/2.5km, the path runs through piles of old millstones – relics of a lost industry. At this point, watch for a path heading off to the right. This leads down to join Long Causeway at a stile, just above a small wood.

Turn right down the track to join the public road at Dennis Knoll car park, then left along the road to return to the start.

A path through the moorland at the foot of a line of rocks and cliffs, with a return passing an old fort and a dramatic tor. Length: 3¹/₂ miles/ 5.5km; Height Climbed: 410ft/125m.

Burbage Rocks is a southern continuation of Stanage Edge; a line of broken, craggy rocks which attracts a lot of rock climbers. To reach it, find the village of Hathersage, by the River Derwent. From the village, take the minor road (it starts as School Lane) which ultimately leads through Ringinglow to Sheffield. Follow this for three miles to reach the twin car parks in the moorland on either side of the Burbage Brook. Either car park will do, but the walk starts from the one beyond the bridge.

There are two signposted footpaths heading south from the road. Take the right-hand one: a clear path running along the foot of the crags.

Follow this path, through heather, grass and bracken, with fallen rocks littering the landscape, until there is a break in the crags to the left. There are two posts by the path. From the second one, a rough path leads down to the right, aiming for the bottom of a conifer wood in the valley.

Cross footbridges – the second an old stone bridge – over two streams below the wood, then climb to the right of the rocks of Carl Wark. Walk to the far end of the rocks then double back to see the wall of the fort and explore the summit.

The higher Higger Tor is clearly visible to the north. Follow the clear

O.S. Sheet 110 (OL 1)

path to the rocks. As you look, you will see a rock on the skyline which appears to have a hole in it. Aim to the left of this to find the easier paths onto the top.

After exploring the tor, take an obvious path back to the car parks.